BASHŌ IN AMERICA

For Janet,

with eternal thanks

for being the gracious
and generous and courageous
leader you are, from one of
your happiest beneficiaries.

With affection always,

Sandy

October 2014

"The spellbinding spirit of the 17th century Japanese poet Matsuo Bashō inhabits these haiku by 21st century poet Sander Zulauf in *Bashō in America*. To read this unique collection, composed on an island in Lake George in the Adirondacks, is to experience a sense of tranquil, even spiritual, closeness to nature, as well as friendship with the human persona of the poet. So much is encompassed and evoked in the few words of each short poem; it is a pleasure to pause between each, letting one's own thoughts invite new possibilities. The poems are honest and open, generous with living detail and wise humor. Living in a cabin on the edge of beautiful water, Zulauf absorbs a creative bond between Bashō and himself, together with American poets such as Thoreau, Whitman, Dickinson and Bishop. Resonant with the past, clear-eyed in the present, Zulauf's *Bashō in America* is a lasting gift with insights relevant for the future."

—Charlotte Mandel, author of *Life Work* (David Roberts Books) and winner of the 2012 New Jersey Poets Prize

BASHŌ IN AMERICA

Haiku by Sander Zulauf

iUniverse

Printed in the United States of America.

Cover photography by Madeline Zulauf.
Japanese cover calligraphy brushed by David A. Heinlein.

iUniverse books may be ordered through booksellers or by contacting:

iUniverse
1663 Liberty Drive
Bloomington, IN 47403
www.iuniverse.com
1-800-Authors (1-800-288-4677)

ISBN: 978-1-4917-4239-6 (sc)
ISBN: 978-1-4917-4240-2 (e)

Library of Congress Control Number: 2014914775

iUniverse rev. date: 09/24/14

For Scott, Dawn, Ella, and Hank—
once more to the lake

ACKNOWLEDGMENTS

Some of these haiku originally appeared in the following publications:

Stillwater Review, U.S. 1 Worksheets, Tiferet Journal, Edison Literary Review, and Exit 13 Magazine.

All interspersed prose quotations by Matsuo Bashō and original translations and quotations by translator/poet Sam Hamill are from *Narrow Road to the Interior and Other Writings* by Matsuo Bashō, translated by Sam Hamill. Copyright © 1998 by Sam Hamill. Reprinted by arrangement with The Permissions Company, Inc., on behalf of Shambhala Publications, Inc., Boston, MA. www.shambhala.com.

Madeline Zulauf patiently listened to all of these haiku on the days they were written and provided the wonderful images for the covers of this book. Herb and Laurel Bergman rented me their "abode of illusion" on an island in Lake George, where most of these poems were born. The County College of Morris provided a much-needed sabbatical for the purpose of writing poetry and working on some translations. Without that gift of one year, this book would have been impossible.

William J. Higginson and Penny Harter's book *The Haiku Handbook,* Robert Hass's *The Essential Haiku,* and Gene Myer's gift to me of Cor van den Heuvel's *The Haiku Anthology* were all indispensible studies before I ever attempted to create my first haiku. Professor David Heinlein, poet, Japanese scholar, and calligraphy artist, assisted in providing haiku translations that became my "transfigurations." I humbly thank my writing professors from long ago—Katherine Kressman Taylor, John Clarke, and Jim Pickering at Gettysburg College in the tumultuous 1960s, and Philip Appleman, Samuel Yellen, Donald Gray, and Philip B. Daghlian at Indiana University in the metamorphosing 1970s. Deborah Cowan and Patricia Crowell graciously guided the Academy of American Poets' Marion Zulauf Poetry Prize at Gettysburg College for decades, for which I am extremely grateful. My friend Marvin Silbersher has been foremost in encouraging me to write and revise my poetry by requesting to hear new work during our frequent phone calls and our impromptu poetry workshops at the Ware House restaurant on Lake Hopatcong. And, of course, I thank Matsuo Bashō, the master of the form, who lived in his own "abode of illusion" on the shores of Japan's Lake Biwa in the 1600s and who made a thousand-mile journey recorded in *Narrow Road to the Interior*—the true inspiration for *Bashō in America.*

once more this afternoon
another thundershower
scatters butterflies

heavy summer rain
punishes the roof
washing away sleep

how foolish!
to think I am
bashō!

maracas at night
(cha-cha-cha) (cha-cha-cha-cha)
august katydids

great horned owl loudly
blesses late summer love songs—
katydids proposing

spider on my pants,
which way
are you going?

autumn morning sun
breaks through rain clouds:
gold beads on pine boughs

lovers in two rooms
dream together
under autumn moon

poet in white habit
writes at her desk long ago—
fathomless courage

fireflies at night
advertise love in july—
meteors ascending

lightning bugs at dusk
fly too slowly to escape
running children's hands

at night in bed
hugging my pillow,
holding my absent wife

thrill of instant grace:
first morning glories abloom
on mailbox trellis

yellow zinnia:
temporary home to
sleeping bumblebee

on the kitchen wall
daddy longlegs reaching out
to touch my finger

crickets, katydids,
river of heaven silenced
by august full moon

headlights to the plane,
we stop for breakfast coffee;
love departs from Newark

moonlight tree shadows—
charcoal sketches painting shades—
daisies, black-eyed susans

opening themselves
into radiant colors
punctuating time

welcome home, bashō,
to abode of illusion—
have a cup of wine

heavy fog at night
a cry pierces the darkness—
owl whistles alone

if only we knew
the peace of cows lying down
in vermont pastures

spider on my porch
spins silk in radial nets
fishing for insects

"Small islands, tall islands pointing at the sky, islands like mothers with baby islands . . . islands cradling islands in the bay . . ."

islands like mothers
with babies—granite shores, green
pines—the mother bunch

"And still a few tiny thatched huts under pines where religious hermits live in tranquility . . ."

pine needles thatch
this cabin's peace, soulful as
the lake's clear waters

"Smoke of burning leaves and pine cones drew me on, touching something deep inside . . ."

smoke of leaves and cones
touches the rising full moon,
wakens sleeping souls

". . . something about Pine Islands . . ."

thin green needles feed
thousands of island pine trees—
brushes on cymbals

"Pine Islands, ah!
Oh, Pine Islands, ah!
Pine Islands, ah!"

"Each poem is the only poem . . . Each moment is the only moment in which one can be fully aware . . . Bashō entered Matsushima by boat in June 1689 and was so taken by its beauty that he declared it to have been made by Oyamazumi, god of the mountains."

waters wholly clear
"lake of the blessed sacrament"
earthly paradise!

"pathos inherent in the beauty of the outer world, a beauty inexorably fated to disappear together with the observer . . ." (Ivan Morris on The Tale of Genji)

beauty this moment
meant to disappear with me
and last forever

in midcentury
by launch to the pine islands
between great mountains

lake waters so clear
seeing bottom way deep down
round white sunfish nests

this bay's holy water
seeing bottom way deep down—
boyhood paradise

boat wakes crash on rocks
long after roars disappear—
mystic crescendos

". . . the journey itself is home . . ."

holding your hand
one final time, melting
away with tears

with you once again
spincasting from the canoe
into the green bay

clouds and rain, lightning!
nothing can get in the way
of the joy i feel

" . . . Bashō was struggling to achieve a resonance between the fleeting moment and the eternal, between the instant of awareness and the vast emptiness of Zen . . ."

from the far island,
a plaintive eastern pewee
asks if we're here

early morning rain
the eastern pewee's cry
floats between islands

that plaintive mercy
listen—there—do you hear it?
sympathetic song

antlers riding waves
a buck swims to the island,
climbs out, disappears

". . . enlightenment as transparent as moonlight . . . reverence and compassion shining in everything it touches . . . its blessing flows down from these mountains, enriching all our lives . . . its light infinitely increasing . . . spreading from hermitage to mountain-top and back . . ." (Feather Black Mountain)

blessings flow from black
mountain down on these islands
to the ready soul

" . . . Gassan, who purified himself with holy water here . . ."

each immersion in
this holy water, ritual
purification

autumn equinox,
who will see these turning leaves
trimming tongue mountain?

full harvest moon
rises above black mountain
lighting pine islands

how many rain clouds
ascended and descended
these green mountainsides?

last of summer's sun
taking the long days with it
into autumn lake

father murphy's shrine—
in the eye of the needle,
beaver builds his hutch

legendary rains
drumming mists through canvas roofs:
boys and girls asleep

at the narrows
the great blue heron flies
over the resting place

two alone fishing
all day in a rented boat
enjoying cold beer

high above the lake
surrounding all the islands:
the river of heaven

autumn on the way
eating cold watermelon
spitting out the pits

in the grandparents'
empty tent, no grandchildren
singing

flashlight at night fell
down fork island outhouse—
laughter, truth, and light

cricket, why do you
stop singing when i come near,
start when i have passed?

absent fourteen summers,
how impossible to say
this is my true place

heavy clouds descend;
black mountain disappears;
two lost children too

drifting into sleep
pixie watkinson opens
vegas ballet school

last night she scrubbed up
three potatoes for dinner . . .
this song is for her

pine island perfume
clings to the cicada's song
like hot summer sun

lying down one summer
adrift in my canoe
reading brave new world

walking near the lake
emily shyly beckons,
holding indian pipes

please anoint my head
with lake george holy waters
now and forever

sunrise lake music
wavelets splash against the rocks
children's sweet singing

haze on the mountain
veil of sheer curtains receives
the loon's morning song

why waste time buying
gold coins? the sun's lake mirror
gives you all you need

can it be possible?
black feather mountain and
black mountain are one?

pines in snowfall
on icebound winter islands
only crows will see

". . . the first task for each artist is to overcome the barbarian or animal heart and mind, to become one with nature . . ."

at black mountain point
fishing in the rain with him—
*ouananiche**

**ouananiche—from Canadian French, from Montagnais, wananish, "landlocked salmon."*

a heron! how lucky
to see it flying over
fourteen mile island

"do you know the name
of that yellow butterfly?"
i said leaves of grass

from a rotting bench
made of logs covered with moss,
pine seedlings growing

upon black mountain
unseen beneath the fire tower
buddha enters nirvana

journey to the lake
the world well lost to us
wanderers through life

cabin of thoreau
pond abode of illusion
henry and bashō

i will wait all night
to see the pine shadows at dawn
greet the living God

queen anne's lace
blossoms in the little waves
at the water's edge

pine trees shed brown
needles while I shed white hairs—
theirs will grow back green

singing campfire songs
fills me with new anguish
for those lost singers

temporary homes
for pursuing happiness
these island campsites

". . . and that is why, even now, after a thousand years, the waves meet this shore with such a melancholy song . . ."

done with my journey,
only my dreams will occupy
my old island homes

now i see her face
abandoned, dying alone,
dawn her final friend

it takes strong will
and great courage to live
at peace and apart

when i realized
i snared fish with their hunger,
i stopped fishing

one clock's ten fifteen,
another eight fifty four—
which do I believe?

in a few minutes
we will make breakfast, or love,
if i am lucky

ah! breakfast! scrambled
eggs, home-fried baked potatoes!
very good. not lucky.

when i found bashō's
lake biwa on the internet
bashō found lake george

cabin's filling up—
bashō   thoreau   kenneth burke
whitman   ginsberg   wright

why this late summer
have i become an old man—
eagle in the clouds

icy lake water
in my cupped hands surprises
my old aching soul

tiny fingerlings—
sunfish, bluegills—swim with me,
calm and curious

another sad truth—
everyone at last goes home—
autumn killer frost

it is so cold
even the silver wind chimes
shiver icy tones

here now on lake george
how i long for old lake george
when the heron flies

tonight the cold wraps
around us as if we dove
deep into the lake

sunlight on the pines
illuminates each needle,
each one praising God

stars floated away
in the bright morning sunlight:
now comes good sailing

a trophy blonde riding
with him in his speedboat—
jack, you'd better think

autumn frost, james
and emily here, flowers
finish knowing now

this week's journey ends
my nerves shaky as a dog
climbing from the lake

one cloud trailing north
through the narrows—miss bishop's
"carded horse's tail"

but for a hammer
thudding a dock far across
the lake, not a sound

september wavelets
babble softly, nervously,
kids' first day of school

thin ice trims the shore
bound to happen—we'll grow old
together waiting

big dipper from
this cabin's porch brings comfort—
ah, the brilliant stars!

twelve billion stars
sparkle human finiteness
beauty on the earth

as our journey ends,
grandchildren ripe with promise—
theirs just beginning

spider in between
cabin window and screen, you seem
to love it here too

coffee now ice-cold
in the white mug I brought out
hot minutes ago

in strong wind and waves
two dead fathers living on
william and joseph

joe brought us summers,
watched his sons becoming men,
counting me as one

i could not do what
they did, midcentury fathers—
divorce ruins kids

can i continue
to write far from here, no pines
exhaling in sun?

georgia at the hyde—
mystic paintings of lake george—
i don't want to leave

now all wakes that break
along this rocky shore
are saying " . . . peace . . . peace . . ."

"*Bashō in America* is a dazzling delight of exquisite haiku. A master of 21st century haiku, Sander Zulauf does something really rare and exceptional in this book. The way he works in writers like Thoreau, Burke, Wright and Ginsberg is especially startling, as is the way he raises the ordinary (like potatoes and breakfast) to the level of the extraordinary. I can think of no other recent book of modern haiku that I loved as much as *Bashō in America*."

—*Laura Boss*, author of *Flashlight* (Guernica Editions) and Editor of *Lips*.

"For a little book of haiku, Sander Zulauf's *Bashō in America* has the capacity for the earth and the sky. Zulauf lassoes the landscape and runs it through the heart. These poems are spacious and precise at once—and this book makes a good companion for a conscious journey, whether outward or inward."

—*BJ Ward*, author of *Jackleg Opera: Collected Poems, 1990 to 2013* (North Atlantic Books).

“‘*how foolish! / to think i am / bashō!*’ Sander Zulauf says in one of the poems early in his collection of haiku. But why not be that kind of foolish? In his case, it produces a beautiful book of moments—pine needle moments, katydid maracas music moments, fishing in a rented boat enjoying cold beer moments, thud of hammer repairing a dock coming across the quiet lake moments, starry night moments. Most of the poems have that kind of image-based elliptical particularity which is the specialty of haiku—the big underlying, overarching truth only gestured at. But here and there he also scatters poems that come right out and say it, and when he uses a word like ‘paradise,’ it is both clear and earned. Like I say, it is a beautiful book.”

—*Howard Nelson*, author of
All the Earthly Lovers (FootHills Publishing).

ABOUT THE AUTHOR

Sander Zulauf is editor emeritus of the *Journal of New Jersey Poets* (1989–2012) and an editor of *The Poets of New Jersey: From Colonial to Contemporary* (Jersey Shore Publications). In addition to editing the first ten volumes of the *Index of American Periodical Verse* (1973–1982), Zulauf has written several books of poetry, which include *Succasunna New Jersey* (Breaking Point), *Living Waters* (St. Dunstan's), and *Where Time Goes* (Dryad Press). He served as editor of Joe Salerno's two posthumous books of poetry, *Dream Paintings from the Heaven of Obscurity* and *Only Here. Bashō in America* and Zulauf's translation of *Veinte poemas de amor y una canción desesperada* (*Twenty Love Poems and a Song of Despair*) by Pablo Neruda (a sensational book first published in Chile in 1924, when Neruda was a twenty-year-old university student) were completed while on sabbatical leave from County College of Morris, where he has been teaching English and creative writing since 1973. A Geraldine R. Dodge poet since 1987, he was named the first poet laureate of the Episcopal Diocese of Newark by Bishop John S. Spong in 1999. He is married to the photographer Madeline Zulauf, whose work graces the cover of this book.

CPSIA information can be obtained at www.ICGtesting.com
Printed in the USA
BVOW04s0217141014

370376BV00001BA/2/P